The SUNDIAL

Elizabeth Lavers

The SUNDIAL

Elizabeth Lavers

Published by Easy Balance Books in conjunction with Writersworld, this book is produced entirely in the UK, is available to order from most book shops in the United Kingdom, and is globally available via UK-based Internet book retailers.

ISBN: 978-0-9572053-9-0

Cover Design by Martin Shute in collaboration with Jag Lall

Copy editor: Sue Croft

WRITERSWORLD

2 Bear Close, Woodstock,

Oxfordshire

OX20 1JX

United Kingdom

Tel 01993 312500

www.writersworld.co.uk

The text pages of this book are produced via an independent certification process that ensures the trees from which the paper is produced comes from well managed sources that exclude the risk of using illegally logged timber while leaving options to use post-consumer recycled paper as well.

Dedication

For Brian, always my hero,
and all the Beautiful People

CONTENTS

ART APPRECIATION

WORK IN PROGRESS

Focus the mind, leaving all else aside;
Take up your pen and await the mysterious sign;
Your reward may be a great winged horse to ride –
More often, one tantalising, limping line.
But capture your infant poem on the wing,
Weave a fine coat of words for it to wear,
Nurture it till its vibrant voice can sing,
And let it go, singing, into the listening air.
It will fly away – to vanish without trace
Or become the song in everybody's mouth?
A common currency in time and place,
Or a disregarded page, blown north and south?
Ignored or learned by heart, loved or unknown,
Once freed, the poem is not yours alone.

WINDOW ON THE RIVER

Tide is surging in now, under the cover of darkness.

Ripples are wearing smart livery, silver and black,

Sliding without pause behind the stone piers of the
bridge,

Hastening upstream about their mysterious affairs.

The bridge itself is seen to be gliding downstream,

Aloof and majestic, defying all possible odds –

But bound to be back before dawn. No people. No birds.

Only the sounds of dark water murmuring and chuckling,

According never a glance at the sovereign moon.

HEATWAVE

The city gasps like a fish. For too many days
It ignored scorching temperatures, tried to run as before;
Now, overwhelmed, it has to face up to defeat.
In the parks, people and dogs sprawl under the trees;
Leaves droop wearily, dustily, losing their shine;
The grass, toasted golden, could be a mown country meadow;
Giggling girls in bright dresses lick melting ice-creams.
In the squares, the respectable dabble bare feet in the fountains;
Parched flowers wilt in containers, dreaming of shade.
Guards swelter in uniforms, schoolchildren toil their way home,
Road surfaces soften, nostalgically smelling of tar.
The sun strikes sparks from the river, sheet lightning from cars.
Recklessly welcomed, intemperate heat holds us fast –
And the city, besieged, keeps a look-out for rescuing rain.

NATURE RAMBLE

They're dressed for action. Two straight backs
Hill-walking boots and tidy hair;
Matching knapsacks and anoraks;
A neat and competent-looking pair

It can cost hours, some simple mistake –
The plan is consulted, stowed once more;
Confident now of the way to take,
As one they head for the nearest door.

Who knows what it is they are here to see,
Or whether they frequently come this way?
Content in each other's company,
They follow their route through the V&A.

ART APPRECIATION

Gaggles of ladies, some still quite young,
(Lipsticks rose madder or crimson lake,
Bright ropes of beads, scarves jauntily flung)
Are enjoying a gossipy coffee break.

So good to share the insights today
Of that – frankly – gorgeously handsome guide!
And the art of the pastry-cook comes into play,
Now the hunger for culture is satisfied.

We must have time to visit the shop –
I want a postcard to send to Fred.
It's been lovely, but now I'm ready to drop –
Does anyone fancy more coffee instead?

PORTRAIT of THREE ARTISTS

An interesting task, to paint those three –
such differing types, clothes, ages, shades of skin –
yet there's some connecting bond, a unity,
but no pecking order. Where should one begin?

There is about them all a modest pride,
an air of wearing laurels, a quiet glow,
as if they are surprised and gratified;
perhaps each has a picture in the show.

One wears a cashmere sweater (neatly shod;
wide gesturing; face and hands are indoor-pale).
The others laugh appreciatively, and nod
as he concludes some entertaining tale.

The youngest, hardly more than a grown lad,
has a well-brushed thatch of curly hair,
a fresh complexion. (The portraitist will add
the scarf coiled in the helmet by his chair.)

Their companion may have stepped straight off a boat;
(tanned, broad shouldered, amiable but tough.)
He lays aside his trusty windproof coat,
ready should inland weather turn out rough.

And here you are, returning from the queue,
with salads, wine, and chunks of wholemeal bread;
seating yourself, you screen them from my view –
and I am content to look at you instead.

THE PERFECT VASE

Selected to be displayed on well-lit shelves
In marble halls and spacious, lofty rooms,
Faultlessly shaped and balanced in themselves,
These perfect vases have no need of blooms.

Thrown - glazed - fired - painted by a master hand,
Unblemished by the passing of the years,
With mirrored reflection and a rosewood stand,
Their timeless beauty brings one close to tears.

And if one also likes to feast one's eyes
On fresh-picked snowdrops - primroses - sweet peas,
Then something understated, small in size,
Perhaps a plain glass jar, is best for these.

They bless a kitchen with their unspoiled grace,
Set in a mug or well-washed mustard pot:
All beauty requires its own particular space,
And a flower is a lovesome thing, God wot.

HEAD OVER HEELS

I can't tell why you love me -
but I know why I love you:
from the moment that I met you
there was nothing else to do.

No weighing in the balance.
No bargaining with fate.
Nobody else worth waiting for,
no matter how long the wait.

No playing any double game,
no hedging any bets,
no other pebbles on the beach.
no doubts, and no regrets.

No, no two ways about it,
no shadow of a mistake;
the roads I choose to travel
are the roads you choose to take.

TIME OUT OF MIND

WORKING ENVIRONMENT

A quiet morning while they lift the boat
and cradle her gently, with the utmost care;
then the inspection, making detailed note
of any little blemish to repair.

The cafe - bliss - is empty but for me,
a waiter, and the smell of baking tart;
I'm quickly served a fragrant pot of tea.
Pen and paper ready. Time to start.

But now the music, right on cue, begins –
a calypso with its vibrant, tropic beat,
soft but pervasive; and that rhythm wins –
my own song is unable to compete.

Outside the windows, chilly water gleams
and wheeling seabirds crisscross in their flight;
inside the kitchen, Caribbean dreams,
steel drums and saxes, colour, warmth and light.

It could be stopped. I might go to complain,
pleading my work, spoil everybody's day;
or march off, into the cold and drizzling rain;
or listen to the music …

Play, man, play!

HIGH GROUND

Up here,
no mere stone wall can tame the wind.
Painfully tingling, chilled ears snuggle deeper
into their warm woollen hat. Altitude and clear air
　make distance deceptive, far near.
Down there,
a cold-water breeze sweeps up and carries bright leaves
streaming along the valley, then allows them to fall.
Opposite,
the lush meadows are swathes of green silk
scattered with scraps of white paper;
the bleating of sheep travels across to us. There's not a
　house to be seen.
Suddenly, a whirlwind of snow-white confetti
rises and eddies above the slow-moving flock,
resolves itself into seabirds – lifts – and is gone.

AMBUSH

At the high point, with two views of the cradling sea
round this small island, chickens control the road
in a blatant extortion racket. Footpads, or worse,
Amazon bandits - not ordinary hens -
flaunting bright, glossy feathers, strong, handsome legs,
they hold to ransom startled visitors.
A mistake, it turns out, to linger to admire
with pockets devoid of any offerings.
They flutter shoulder high to attack an ear,
peck viciously at ankles, hands and shins.
No people about. One solitary cow
without a glance goes slowly sauntering on.
The strangers turn tail and flee to the friendly shore.
In the welcoming teashop, bird food is for sale.

HEBRIDEAN SEA SONG

Some keep an eye on the sea-charts to plot where we may be;
The unending chain of islands unwinds. I am all at sea.
Beautiful, unyielding, inhospitable terrain;
Cliffs and rocky outcrops softened by falling rain.
A clear light, always changing with the ever-changing view;
Mist rises, and grey waters are a deep and vivid blue.
A shaft of distant sunshine falls on some lonely bay;
The golden light of evening graces the close of day.

And the voices go on singing
Their sweet and plangent songs,
Of love, and love's betrayal,
And remembered, ancient wrongs.

ISLAND BUS RIDE

Clear day – island view – salt spray – sky
blue,

Low tide – seabird flocks – horizon wide –
yellow rocks;

Spirits high – long strand – mackerel sky –
white sand

Gulls mew – gliding free – skimming blue-
green sea.

Offshore – mares' tails – bright spinnakers –
white sails;

Summer showers – potent drink – wild flowers –
sea pink;

Coloured kites flying high – poet's delight –
red sky.

Lots of pots on window ledges – sunny spots
and flowering hedges;

Homeward bound – curves and bends – familiar
ground

                 and journey ends.

VOYAGING THE NIGHT

Most yachts, like birds, fold their white wings at dusk;

cargo-vessels and tankers keep rumbling along,

and cruise-shops, large or small, tend to voyage the night.

When the noise of the rowdiest revellers is dying away,

as bars close, music stops, cabins all fall asleep,

the bridge, quiet brain of the ship, springs into fresh life –

heartbeat of the engines quickens, the anchor comes up,

yesterday's port falls astern.

Daylight lies far ahead.

Sea lanes, thronged with shipping, form a conduit for news,

an intangible network of lighted symbols and voices,

communicating in detail. Steady as she goes.

Stars are alive, the sea sparkles, moon silvers the waves

until the sky fades and up swings a red and gold sun:

and the Captain exchanges a smile with his sweetheart,
  the sea.

THISTLES and GROUSE

John o' Groats, porridge oats, fishing floats, castle moats,
Cannot find my nature notes, I'll simply have to bluff.

Gorse and heather, scuffed boot leather, misty weather,
stick together,
Can this be an eagle's feather? Going's very rough.

Up and down the rocky ridges, swatting at a million
midges,
Bogs and burns, no handy bridges, Billy Goats Gruff.

Hill walking, deerstalking, No talking, Paths forking,
When can we go back to Dorking? Blind Man's Bluff.

Tired of tramping prickly stubble, welcome end to toil
and trouble:

Single malt? Make that a double – which may not be
enough!

TIME OUT OF MIND

She has long outlived all those who shared her youth,
and she is old, has been old for decades;
one frail white hand rests on the upholstered arm
of the green chair, protective carapace.

"Such a quiet lady, very little trouble.
By the look of things, she has drifted off again."

No, not adrift! Voyaging remembered seas,
competent, alert, and alive to the here and now –
sea-swell, wind strength, the warmth of the morning sun.
No one knows her whereabouts, when she'll return.
Single-handed in fair weather, far offshore,
no other ships. She reaches to trim the sail,
consults the chart weighted with a smooth white stone,
glances up at the fleecy, scudding clouds.
Her hands on the wheel are business-like, tanned, strong,
the nails cut short. A turtle swims slowly past,
on its way from who knows where to who knows where.
High cries of seabirds. Rhythmic lift of waves.
Salt spray. Her trusty and familiar boat.
The ocean in all its glory belongs to her.
Unheard and happy, she lifts her clear voice, and sings.

NIGHT FLIGHT

Darkened cabin. No one else awake.

Steady background hum of engine noise.

Softly raised, the blind reveals endless night,

the plane hanging motionless among the stars

while the uncharted earth rolls widdershins,

self-absorbed, majestically slow.

Perhaps more sleep? . . . Faint tremor in the wing . . .

An excited quiver. Hunter scenting game,

Stealthily I take a look outside.

A dazzling moon has painted the darkness white.

Below us, snow and mountains, jagged peaks,

stretch on and on in glittering, savage splendour,

a vast and secret world. No villages, no fires, no lighted
lamps

The moon, the snow,

        and no one else to witness and record.

ON THE WATER

Boats raise eager heads like warhorses hearing
the trumpet,

Sniffing the freshening breeze, impatient to be
on their way;

Untethered, they move off sedately, in a long
line astern,

Out through the harbour mouth, ready to kick up
their heels;

Water hisses under their bows as the sails rattle
up.

Yachts in their various classes make ready to
race;

Others curve smartly away, heading for a new
port,

This side of the water or that, or are doing
speed trials,

Crews testing their knowledge and skill against
wind and tide.

Black jet-skis, like gangsters' motorbikes, power
about,

The envy of little boys watching from safe
vantage points,

While water-skiers drive chariots out from the
beaches,

Swooping and gliding, triumphant, riding the
waves.

FULL HOUSE

VISITORS' BOOK

"You are the best of good fellows,
and you are the people we prize -
hospitable, warm-hearted, witty,
talented, modest and wise.
You are the flowers in life's
meadows
and the brightest of stars in our
skies."

SNOWDROPS

Tenderest green and white
Beneath lowering skies of grey –
Surely too clean, too slight
To have pierced through the heavy clay.

Fragile, like finest silk,
Causing the heart to lift;
Scattered like drops of milk,
Each a delicate, precious gift.

In the cold wind, bells swinging low,
They gracefully sway and bend,
Maintaining, come frost, come snow,
All winters, at last, must end.

CALL TO ARMS

Keep watching, waiting, until, at last, it comes –
that longed-for moment when one daffodil
bends its green head to sound a golden horn,
alerting the rest.
                  Reinforcements are at hand,
but Winter's rearguard action is hard fought –
cold winds, cold nights, cold mornings, bitter frosts.
Spring emerges triumphant, that one small band
grown to an army of massed daffodils.
With jubilant birdsong heard from every twig,
hillsides carpeted with grass and flowers,
candles alight in each horse-chestnut tree,
the earth rejoices, now that the field is won.

MAY DAY OBSERVED

Ice particles sparkle in gusts of pure Arctic air,

Green and white snowdrops have just reluctantly, gone,

But bold yellow clusters of daffodils still catch the eye.

Flurries of snowflakes fall lightly on red-flowering may;

Primroses grow among bluebells in ravishing hues –

(The shade of Vermeer picks up an invisible brush

and seizes his palette.) The earth itself seems surprised

To see dandelions, daisies and cuckoo-flowers brave frosts
together.

White-blossoming blackthorn lights up dark corners of
                                                    woodland

And punctuates scribbled lines of bare, leafless hedges.

Warm winds from the south are predicted to reach us
tomorrow.

GREEN GRASS

The rain has stopped, after washing the green grass
greener.

A young doe with her little twins at foot

feasts on apples fallen from the tree;

a family scrumping outing. Moorhens and ducks

await their turn to indulge. Green woodpeckers, heads
cocked

give ants' nests their earnest attention. A few raindrops
hang,

ephemeral jewels, on rose bushes. Peaceful and calm,

at least for this moment in time, snails, wasps, butterflies,

and all the rest, go about their various occasions,

undisturbed by the naiad at home in the clear, chilly
water.

THE SUNDIAL

Monumental and gilded, placed on a south-facing wall,

Great sundials are seen on cathedrals, on a castle, or a town hall

But Martin keeps his in a pocket, brimful of sunshine and light,

(A sextant is kept in another, to plot his position at night.)

Each is a beautiful object, lovingly, cunningly made,

With elegance wedded to function, as in any good tool for a
trade.

The domestic, familiar version, at its best on long, summer days,

Hardly noticed at home in the garden, comes to life in the sun's
friendly rays.

But perhaps my favourite sundial is the simplest I've ever
found –

A strong, straight stick, standing upright, and driven well into
the ground;

It timed the shared irrigation between plots of land, one by one;

The shadow was both judge and jury – no one out-argues the
sun.

It stood by the channels of water in a green village, humming
with bees,

Set in a parched desert landscape, but fruitful, and shaded with
trees.

SEXTANT

'At sunset, aim a hand's breadth above the horizon to allow for the curvature of the earth.'

At school it was called Trigonometry
And attracted me, to my surprise;
A surprise, too, for the class teacher,
Unused to the gleam in my eyes.

It took us outside the classroom
To measure the height of the school,
With our bits of string stuck to protractors,
With sine and cosine for our rule.

My thoughts often veered off at tangents
When maths seemed of no mortal use –
But here, I could hardly believe it,
Was fun with the hypotenuse!

But now, look with care at the sextant
In its solid and seaworthy box;
Not made for a lark in the playground,
But to keep a real ship off the rocks.

Beautiful, vital equipment,
Held in a competent hand
To pinpoint a speck in the ocean,
A thousand miles from the land.

WILLIAM IN THE APPLE ORCHARD

You are cutting the lush, sweet-smelling orchard grass,
an extravaganza of blossom overhead,
a riot of pinks and whites and ecstatic birds.
Shafts of Spring sunshine, slanting between trees,
illuminate daisies, buttercups, a rake,
glint on the great scythe, borrowed from Old Father
                                    Time.
The ancient skill is second nature now,
your grip on polished handles confident,
the wide sweep rhythmic, economical,
reaping broad swathes. Occasionally you pause,
perhaps let the whetstone whisper along the blade.
A good morning's work; and now time to go in for lunch.

FULL HOUSE

The family's in residence, how fortunate I am!
There are toast crumbs in the butter and butter in the jam,
coffee mugs beneath the sofa and a heap of coats on top,
five different kinds of music – very loud and doesn't stop.
The window catch is broken – must have taken quite a pull –
the larder's always empty and the laundry basket full,
boots scattered in the hallway, not all of them in pairs,
socks for several centipedes and mud all up the stairs.
I can tell they're back from jogging by the slamming of the door
and the singing in the shower, and the wet towels on the floor.
They burst with bounding energy and constant merriment,
and quite outrageous anecdotes and, "That's not what I meant,"
with interruptions, laughs and groans, and "Pass those biscuits,
                                                        please",
end-of-the-rainbow travel plans, and "Is there any cheese?"
and news of friends, their broken legs, or hearts, and on and on …
and I know we're going to miss them, the instant they are
                                                        gone.

AU REVOIR

Long-drawn-out doorstep farewells, and dashes indoors
for the dog's lead – forgotten toy – coat from the
back door – a book.

At last, off they go, waving madly. Come again soon!
It has been brilliant! Go safely!

A calm silence falls

and at once the listening house seems to double in size,

though the faraway clock, softly chiming, is clear as a
bell.

Once the laundry is dealt with, the kitchen swept clean,

an unwonted neatness sets in.

You can hear yourself think –

There's work to be done, plans to make, and letters to
write.

Peace and quiet can be good things.

In moderation, of course.

FORBIDDEN FRUIT

In Eden, forbidden but tempting,
And never named in the Good Book,
A fruit quite distinct from all others –
Not something Eve needed to cook.

So who says that it was an apple?
A chorus of voices, or one?
Why not a pear, a ripe mango,
Or a luscious peach warmed by the sun?

It's an innocent pleasure, thank Heaven,
To enjoy an apple a day,
Selecting one's favourite flavour
Perhaps cooked a traditional way.

Egremont, Braeburn, Pink Lady –
Not racehorses but apple trees;
Lord Derby and Rosemary Russet . . .
Even Eden might envy us these.

CRABAPPLE TREE

Fruits hang in bright asymmetry,
Small perfect apples against the grey
Of clouds, tossed like a wintry sea
By winds that whisk the leaves away;

Their vivid colours brighter turn,
Mimicking eastern artistry:
And lacquered reds and crimsons burn
On the fine lines of the ink-black tree.

ISOBEL, HEAD GARDENER

Pleasant to sit on this bench, my bones warmed by the sun;
There are soothing lawn-mower noises two gardens away,
A waft of cut grass and a twittering of birds.
That shrub does quite well, surviving drought and neglect,
But I move it close to the lavender hedge in my mind.
Real gardening is hard work, and its own reward, too;
It has a contemplative side, restoring one's balance
As one plants and prunes and pots on.
Laborare est Orare – Work is Prayer –
But the flesh grows weak, however ardent the spirit.
Footballers become managers, top ballerinas
Teachers of dance. Gardeners, as they age,
Move into garden-design, once the back and the knees
Come out on strike, reckon they've done quite enough.
If I were to kneel by that border, trowel in hand,
I'd never stand up again without someone's help,
With encouraging murmurs from them, and loud groans from
                                                    me:
Not to be thought of. It's notebook and catalogues now –
But I miss the feel of damp earth, the soil under my nails.
House plants? Yes, of course - but not, shall we say, the real
                                                    thing.

THE IRIS

A challenge to select one flower for you
From all those you have painted, loved and grown,
But then, of course – 'to thine own self be true' –
You name your own.

The bearded iris you so firmly choose
Is like you, tall and upright, straight and strong,
And opens to reveal rich, rainbow hues.
It sings your song.

Yet irises have landlocked lives to live,
While you go ocean-wide adventuring;
From the water's edge, they wave prayer-flags and give
Blessings as you take wing.

HEART OF OAK

Mellowed, and blending with the countryside,
The Sussex house is built of local brick
From vanished kilns in nearby villages.
Indoors, the panelling, beams and banisters
Are older, made of rock-hard, seasoned oak
Recovered from our decommissioned ships,
Then put to fresh use, these many miles inshore.
Names of the ships, their provenance? Unknown.
Yet when night-time comes, in the quiet hours of
                                              the dark
The wind sings sweetly of the waves and tides;
And stairs and cupboard doors stir in their sleep,
Making the comfortable creaks and sighs,
The muffled cracks and groans of ships at sea.
By daybreak, the house has sailed back to its place,
Keeping its counsel, treasuring its dreams.

CABINET MAKER

His workshop smells of sawdust, and hot glue
Boiled up for use in its sinister black pot.
His shining tools are ready to his hand,
Called by their names: awl, hammer, jigsaw, plane,
Chisel, gouge, drill-bits, vice and clamps.
The great brass-bound spirit-level – not a toy.
Sandpaper, coarse and fine; glass-paper, finer yet.
Things finished seem made of the stuff of dreams,
Too perfect to be the work of human hands.
The child plays in the fragrant curls of wood
Under the workbench. Offcuts, large or small,
Are trains or boats or aeroplanes or cars.
The atmosphere is peaceful, calm, content.
A good place to be. They exchange an occasional word.

In the kitchen, cooking, cleaning, drinking tea,
The women gossip endlessly all day.
The child pays no attention, eating cake, until:
"Someone must tell him. It's time he gave up the shed."
"Yes, but what about all that clobber? And all his tools?"
"Well, I certainly wouldn't want them dumped on me."

FOR THOSE OF RIPER YEARS

The human mind was not designed
to laze, inert and dull,
ignoring poor, perplexed mankind
and skulking inside its skull.

Nor should the brain grow soft and drain
like a fruit fallen to the ground,
while cures for a problem or a pain
are waiting to be found.

So, if the cap fits, while time permits,
plot a path through the moral maze;
brush up your talents and sharpen your wits;
you may yet set the world ablaze.

INDOLENCE and SLOTH

In order not to become addicted,
Avoid all indolence and sloth;
I find to my shame I am afflicted,
Not with one of them but with both.

So many things out there to do
If only one managed to fit them in;
Getting started is hard, it's true -
And so is choosing where to begin.

Just living seems to take all day,
Rising and falling with the tide;
Perhaps I'll review the state of play,
Later; quite when, I can't decide.

I really don't mean to waste my time
Too lazy even to reach for a pen,
A bone-rotten idle, despicable crime.
I will do better; but I don't know when.

EXPLETIVE FREE ZONE

A lady does not curse and swear,
No matter what, no matter where;
Whatever problem has occurred
She won't use language best unheard,
Nor oaths that cause a startled hush
And make the saltiest sailor blush -
(Though she may shriek and tear her hair
When things are very hard to bear.)
But me no buts, if me no ifs,
A lady never blinds nor stiffs,
But pursues a policy of perfection …

We permit the occasional exception.
We all could mention one or two,
Or (let's be honest), quite a few.

CHAMELEON

Do not be misled. Truth comes in no simple guise –
It is a chameleon, blending with varying hues,
To a beholder, blood-red, green, orange, true blue,
Depending on viewpoint, or where he chooses to stand.
Despotic regimes dictate it, to save time and trouble,
Rewriting history, stamping out queries and quibbles.
Pity that hard-pressed chameleon when power changes
                                    hands,
An instant adaptation to very different stripes,
With no tell-tale traces remaining of what has been hard
                                    fact.
'Truth is beauty, beauty truth,' someone mutters,
But the chameleon is ugly, reptilian, and swivel-eyed,
With a cold, dispassionate gaze. Don't venture close –
Its tongue is a swift and deadly, a far-reaching weapon,
An ambush for the unwary fluttering near.
Camouflage is the name of its game. You need sharp eyes
And that's the truth. Yet there are other truths,
Not all of them written in water or on the sea sand.

ODDS & EVENS

MAGIC GARDENS

You may not quite believe me
However hard you try,
But I have a magic garden,
Right up in the sky.

High above the city,
Away from the dust and noise,
In among the flowers
I play with my favourite toys.

And I know another garden
With a truly magic swing,
Where coloured pheasants walk about
And tiny robins sing.

WATERLILY

Sometimes I think I'd like to be
A mermaid underneath the sea,
Sitting on smooth rocks in the sand,
A silver mirror in my hand.

I do love swimming, it is true,
But then I love my skateboard, too;
Perhaps I wouldn't really wish
To be half me and half a fish.

If you like different kinds of fun –
To skip and dance, to jump and run,
Ride a horse, go for a sail –
Two legs are better than a tail.

But when I'm nearly half asleep,
I seem to be there, very deep,
Where pearls and shipwrecked treasures
                                   gleam,
And I'm a mermaid in my dream.

ODDS & EVENS

Whichever numbers anyone draws,
They're either **O**dds or **E**vens;
Mine are not quite as **E**ven as yours,
But not nearly as **O**dd as Stephen's.

There's nothing **O**dd about my **1**,
So easy to draw, a simple stick.
My **2** goes swimmingly, like a swan;
But my **3** looks **O**dd, by some sly trick.

4? An **L** with an extra bit;
My **5** is friendly and wears a hat;
But **3** doesn't seem to want to fit –
My **3** is plain **O**dd, and that is that.

6 and **9** are clearly brothers,
And anybody can draw a **7**;
Plump, happy **8** smiles at the others –
But my **3** is the **O**ddest thing under heaven.

While the **E**ven, uncomplicated dears,
Are sitting pretty and having fun,
3 frowns or sulks or sniffs and sneers,
My **O**dd little **3**, the awkward one.

ARCHIE

Time to move back from Africa,
For the children to start a new school -
Goodbye to the tropical heat and rain,
To friends they may never meet again,
To the music, the drumming no one can explain,
And the afternoons spent in the pool.

Then, "Oh, please, let the parrot come too,
Archie, our African Grey!
He can imitate everything he's ever heard,
To leave him behind would be cruel and absurd,
He's a family member, this talented bird,
We simply can't give him away!"

Forms in quadruple must be filled in,
Rubber stamps required on each page;
And the parrot regarded, with sapient eye,
The purpose-built box in which he would fly
Northward, many miles up in the sky,
With the permit attached to his cage.

But when the day of departure came round,
Not a feather of him could they find;
However they called, he couldn't be traced.
They left for the airport late and in haste.
All that time, all those efforts had just gone to waste,
Parrot, permit and cage left behind.

He had not been the prey of some crafty cat,
Nor kidnapped and smuggled away:
Occasionally is heard on the breeze
Champagne corks popping, a whistle, a sneeze …
And a well-known voice, laughing high in the trees –
It's Archie, the African Grey.

FIRST SUNDIAL

The grown-ups, too busy talking
To lift me up to see,
Cheerfully kept on walking,
Then turned round to call for me.

It told the time? Were they tricking?
I could just see a spike on top –
No sound of any ticking.
Did a sundial ever stop?

No hole for a man to wind it,
Its workings a mystery,
And what a strange place to find it,
In a garden beside the sea.

I thought, 'I can't understand it',
But I knew what I would do;
It's one of the things – I've planned it –
I shall ask when I next see you.

FINE DINING

A family of four out for a treat,
The father proud, his smiling wife content;
Elegance, style, and wonderful things to eat,
A glamorous evening, after a day well spent.

Dazed by long hours afloat and on the beach,
The boy is propping up his heavy head;
Sunburned, sea-scoured, almost beyond speech,
His needs are simple: mounds of food, then bed.

His sister, dressed to kill, through black-rimmed eyes
Glowers about her. Everyone is old …
But no, a young, handsome waiter! Here's a prize
To weave into the tale her friends are told.

The boy wakes up as dishes reach their table;
His sister is poured a glass of sparkling wine;
Fresh fish, prepared as only the chef is able,
Garnished with roast tomatoes on the vine.

And now – dessert! Nine different ice creams!
The meal has reached its real high-water mark.
Coffee and chocolates, the stuff of dreams,
And the stroll home, through the warm and scented dark.

LADY WITH A LUTE

In her embroidered garden, on the green and flower-starred lawn,
Where close to her, on her silken skirts, nestles her little fawn,
The Lady plucks music from a lute with embroidered silver strings,
And her voice rings sweetly on the air, as all alone she sings:

> *"Return to me, my love, why do you stay?*
> *Come back, my dear heart, why so long away?"*

The unicorn stands spellbound; squirrels peep above
From leafy branches hung with fruit; a snowy-feathered dove
And tiny songbirds flutter down, round her embroidered feet,
To hear the Lady singing:

> *"My love, when shall we meet?*
> *Life has no joy without you, night or day;*
> *My heart's own treasure, come to me, I pray."*

And where is her handsome sweetheart? Adrift on perilous seas?
Or captive of some enchantress, in a castle hid in the trees?
Hunting the mighty silver stag? Nobly righting a wrong?
Or does the Lady sing and play because she loves the song?

> *"My constant heart is yours and will not stray*
> *However long and slow your homeward way . . ."*

OLIVIA'S SONG

There's a wide, wide world stretching out under
the sky,

With great cities too far for an eagle to fly,

Mountains too cold for a bear to survive,

And oceans too deep for a dolphin to dive.

There are strange fruits and butterflies, deserts
and springs,

And people and animals, castles and kings,

And jungles too tangled to cut your way through -

So much to discover, and so much to do.

The world goes on forever, but I know where I'll
start:

Take my favourite places, and learn them by
heart.

THE APPLE of DISCORD

When Henry Wilson decided to grapple

With Applied Science, he picked up an apple,

(Like Adam and Eve, and, to mention but few,

All the Three Graces, and yes, Newton, too.)

We gather from an eyewitness report

That the Cider Venture was cut sadly short,

But Henry had certainly got the hang

Of recreating the first Big Bang.

SUNDAY VISITORS

To the keen eye of horse-whisperer Jess
The mysterious ponies seem quite at their ease –
Skewbald Sammy and brave Black Bess –
But how did they get in our field, if you please?

Tails idly swishing, a trespassing pair;
A delight and a worry – let's phone the vet,
The police, the stables and Equine Care –
They are greedily snatching grass far too wet.

Recorded message: RSPCA
Will not collect either horse or cow . . .
We should mend the fence so they cannot stray,
And can't we consider them ours for now?

Ah, but leading Sam, and bareback on Bess,
Comes a stable-hand – horsecoper – brigand chief,
(His job-description is hard to assess),
Bringing disappointment. Mixed with relief.

IN OTHER WORDS

(by request)

STONE FLOWER

In de oudste lagen van mijn ziel,
waar hij van stenen is gemaakt
bloiet als een gaaf fossiel
de stenen bloem van uw gelaat

Ik kan me niet van uw bevrijden,
er bloiet niets in mijn steen dan gij;
de oude weelden zijn voorbij
maar niets kan mij meer van u scheiden

(Margaretha Droogleever Fortuyn-Leenmans)
   M.Vasilis 1909–1998

~

In that stratum of my soul so deep
that it has turned to stone,
blooms your stone-flower left for me to keep,
a perfect fossil in monochrome.

I cannot rid myself of you.
Nothing but you blooms in my stone.
The old abundance is long gone,
but nothing can ever divide us two.

HEUREUX QUI COMME ULYSSE

Heureux qui, comme Ulysse, a fait un beau voyage,
Ou comme cestuy-là qui conquit la toison,
Et puis est retourné, plein d'usage et raison,
Vivre entre ses parents le reste de son âge !

Quand reverrai-je, hélas, de mon petit village
Fumer la cheminée, et en quelle saison
Reverrai-je le clos de ma pauvre maison,
Qui m'est une province, et beaucoup davantage ?

Plus me plaît le séjour qu'ont bâti mes aïeux,
Que des palais Romains le front audacieux,
Plus que le marbre dur me plaît l'ardoise fine :

Plus mon Loir gaulois, que le Tibre latin,
Plus mon petit Liré, que le mont Palatin,
Et plus que l'air marin la doulceur angevine.

Joachim du Bellay, Les Regrets, sonnet XXXI, 1558

THOUGHTS OF HOME

Happy the man who has sailed the seven seas

And then returned, having travelled far and wide,

Like Ulysses, or Jason with his Fleece,

Seasoned and shrewd, to his own countryside.

But I, when shall I see rising above the thatch

The smoke of my own village? At what date

Will my own eyes see, set in its garden patch,

That house more to me than any vast estate?

Dearer to me is my ancestral home

Than all the grandiose palaces of Rome,

Finer than marble our local stone to me;

Loved more than their Tiber my little Loire in Gaul

And the soft airs of Anjou more than the tang of the sea.

LE BONHEUR de ce MONDE

Avoir une maison commode, propre et belle,
Un jardin tapissé d'espaliers odorans,
Des fruits, d'excellent vin, peu de train, peu d'enfans,
Posseder seul sans bruit une femme fidèle,

N'avoir dettes, amour, ni procès, ni querelle,
Ni de partage à faire avecque ses parens,
Se contenter de peu, n'espérer rien des Grands,
Régler tous ses desseins sur un juste modèle,

Vivre avecque franchise et sans ambition,
S'adonner sans scrupule à la dévotion,
Dompter ses passions, les rendre obéissantes,

Conserver l'esprit libre, et le jugement fort,
Dire son chapelet en cultivant ses entes,
C'est attendre chez soi bien doucement la mort.

Christophe Plantin 1520 – 1589

EARTHLY HAPPINESS

A comfortable, well-kept, pleasant house,
A scented garden bright with every hue;
For you alone, a modest, faithful spouse
Fruits, fine wine, small bustle; children few.
No debts, no lovers, lawsuits or disputes,
No relatives with claims on your estate;
Always well-founded plans for your pursuits;
Content, expecting nothing of the great;
Leading life honestly, without ambition;
Taming your passions, keeping them subdued,
Practising piety without inhibition,
Maintaining an open mind and judgement shrewd.
So, saying your prayers while tending orchard trees
You'll live out your days at home, your heart at ease.

CHANSON D'AUTOMNE

Les sanglots longs
Des violons
De l'automne
Blessent mon coeur
D'une langueur
Monotone.

Tout suffocant
et blême, quand
sonne l'heure,
je me souviens
des jours anciens
et je pleure.

Et je m'en vais
au vent mauvais
qui m'emporte
deçà, delà,
pareil à la
feuille morte.

Charles Baudelaire 1759 - 1827

SONG for AUTUMN

Sobbing violins
Played by the winds
Of autumn, make
A wound in my heart
And impart
A dull, lingering ache.

Fighting for breath
And pale as death
When the clock chimes,
My tears fall
As I recall
Past times.

And so I go
Where ill winds blow
Me in my grief,
Here and there
Or anywhere,
Like a dead leaf.

PARFUM EXOTIQUE

Quand, les deux yeux fermés, en un soir chaud d'automne,
Je respire l'odeur de ton sein chaleureux,
Je vois se dérouler des rivages heureux
Qu'éblouissent les feux d'un soleil monotone ;

Une île paresseuse où la nature donne
Des arbres singuliers et des fruits savoureux ;
Des hommes dont le corps est mince et vigoureux,
Et des femmes dont l'oeil par sa franchise étonne.

Guidé par ton odeur vers de charmants climats,
Je vois un port rempli de voiles et de mâts
Encor tout fatigués par la vague marine,

Pendant que le parfum des verts tamariniers,
Qui circule dans l'air et m'enfle la narine,
Se mêle dans mon âme au chant des mariniers.

Charles Baudelaire 1759 - 1827

EXOTIC PERFUME

When I breathe in the scent of your warm breast,
Eyes closed, on mild autumn evenings, I behold
Before me happy, light-dazzled shores unfold,
By a constant fiery sun caressed.
An island of indolence, by nature blessed
With curious trees, fruits which sweet savour hold,
With men of vigour, cast in a slender mould,
And women of startlingly candid eyes possessed.
Your scent to pleasant places pilots me –
A harbour filled with sails and masts I see,
All wearied out by ocean breakers still;
While wafts of the trees' perfume, green tamarind,
Drift through the air, my nostrils fill
And blend with the sailors' shanties in my mind.

LE DORMEUR du VAL

C'est un trou de verdure où chante une rivière

Accrochant follement aux herbes des haillons

D'argent : où le soleil, de la montagne fière,

Luit : c'est un petit val qui mousse de rayons.

Un soldat jeune, bouche ouverte, tête nue,

Et la nuque baignant dans le frais cresson bleu,

Dort ; il est étendu dans l'herbe, sous la nue,

Pâle dans son lit vert où la lumière pleut.

Les pieds dans les glaïeuls, il dort. Souriant comme

Sourirait un enfant malade, il fait un somme :

Nature, berce-le chaudement : il a froid.

Les parfums ne font pas frissonner sa narine ;

Il dort dans le soleil, la main sur sa poitrine

Tranquille. Il a deux trous rouges au côté droit.

Arthur Rimbaud, 1854 - 1891

THE SLEEPER in the VALLEY

A dell filled with greenery. A river, singing,

Hangs random silver scraps on tufted grass.

A little valley, where the sun is flinging

A mesh of sunbeams from the mountain pass.

A soldier, young, lips parted, is asleep;

Bare head, neck lapped by cresses, fresh and blue,

Lying full length in dappled grasses deep,

His green couch bathed in sunshine. Pale of hue,

He sleeps, feet among flowers springing wild,

His smile that of a drowsing, sickly child.

He is cold; in warm Nature's arms let him abide.

Heedless of scented air, he takes his rest

There in the sun, one hand upon his breast,

At peace. He has two red holes in his side.

Printed by: Copytech (UK) Limited trading as
Printondemand-worldwide.com
9 Culley Court, Bakewell Road, Orton Southgate,
Peterborough, PE2 6XD